People and the Sea

A & C BLACK • LONDON

People and the Sea

contents

© Blake Publishing Pty Ltd 2002
Additional Material © A & C Black Publishers Ltd 2003

First published 2002 in Australia by Blake Education Pty Ltd

This edition published 2003 in the United Kingdom by
A&C Black Publishers Ltd, 37 Soho Square, London W1D 3QZ
www.acblack.com

ISBN 0-7136-6601-3

A CIP record for this book is available from the British Library.

Written by Sharon Dalgleish and Garda Turner
Science Consultant: Dr Will Edwards, James Cook University
Design and layout by The Modern Art Production Group
Photos by Photodisc, Stockbyte, John Foxx, Corbis, Imagin,
Artville Digital Vision and Corel

UK Series Consultant: Julie Garnett

Printed in Hong Kong by Wing King Tong Co Ltd

A & C Black uses paper produced with elemental chlorine-free pulp,
harvested from managed sustainable forests.

Explorers

From early times people have set sail on the oceans to explore the unknown. Some explorers looked for new lands to settle. Others looked for adventure, treasure or fame.

More than 3 000 years ago people explored the Pacific Ocean. In small canoes, people used the stars to find their way. By the early 1200s the magnetic compass had been invented. Sailors could then navigate more easily. Even so, the journeys were still filled with danger.

Long before science helped us understand the oceans, people thought the Earth was flat. Sailors believed that if they sailed far enough, they would fall off the edge of the world. Of course they never did, but storms, pirates and hidden reefs meant that some ships did sink to the bottom of the sea. Today, adventurers go in search of the sunken treasure!

Stormy seas and rocky coasts made sailing to new lands dangerous.

Galleons were used as warships and for trade from the 1400s to the 1600s.

Early boats were very simple.

DID YOU KNOW?

Ferdinand Magellan's ships were the first to sail around the world. Magellan set sail from Spain in 1519 with five ships. In 1522 only one of his ships made it home.

Water Pressure

The water pressure in the deep sea is extremely high. Deep-sea water pressure would crush a person.

Try this experiment to see how **water pressure** increases in deeper water.

You will need:
- deep bucket
- straw or plastic tube
- water and food colouring
- balloon
- elastic band

What to do:

1. Fill the bucket with water.

2. Attach the straw or plastic tube to the balloon with an elastic band. Fill the balloon with coloured water.

3. Slowly lower the balloon into the bucket.

4. Watch the level of the coloured water as you push the balloon deeper.

Now try this:

Wrap your hand in a plastic bag and place your hand under the water. You will feel the pressure increase as you push your hand deeper into the water.

Just below the surface, the water pressure is low.

Deeper down, the water pressure pushes the water from the balloon into the tube.

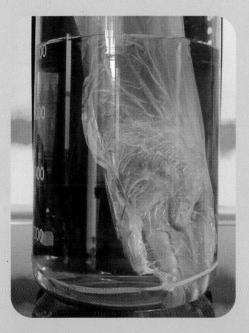

The water pressure presses the plastic around your hand.

Food from the Sea

People have always caught fish and other sea creatures using baskets, hooks and nets. Today, large fishing boats can catch, clean and freeze fish while still at sea.

Modern fishing boats take huge amounts of seafood from the sea. Popular ocean fish that people eat include tuna, herring, sardines, cod and snapper. Every year about 75 million tonnes of fish are caught worldwide.

fishmonger

Seaweed is also **harvested**. People eat it raw or cooked and sometimes use it to thicken foods such as ice-cream and yoghurt. Seaweed can also be used to make toothpaste and sausages!

In some hot countries, people trap sea water in shallow ponds. The sun and wind dry up the water, leaving behind the salt. The salt is collected and used to season and preserve food.

Large fishing boats use a tracking system called sonar, to find large schools of fish.

Many people use small boats to go fishing.

This man is harvesting seaweed.

Energy from the Sea

Almost a quarter of the oil and natural gas we use comes from beneath the sea. Oil and gas are fossil fuels that people use to make heat and power.

Fossil fuels are the remains of long-dead plants and animals that were preserved in a rock-like form. Millions of years ago, plants and tiny sea creatures died and sank to the bottom of the ocean. The plants and animals were slowly pressed together. Then heat and pressure changed them into natural gas or oil.

Geologists drill holes in the ocean floor, looking for oil and gas. When a large amount of oil or gas is found, a platform is built in the open sea. Narrow holes are drilled into the seabed. The oil or gas is then pumped to the surface. Oil is loaded into big ships called tankers. Natural gas is sent to the shore by pipeline.

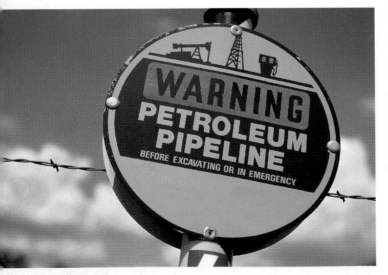

There are large oil platforms in the ocean.

Large pipes carry gas across the land for use or for storage.

These men are drilling for oil on an oil rig.

GO FACTS
DID YOU KNOW?
Oil and gas are running out so the world needs new sources of energy, such as sun and wind.

Working at Sea

If you're looking for an easy time, you may not want to work at sea. Some people think the ocean is a great place to find a career — full of excitement and discovery.

An oil platform is like a small city at sea. Hundreds of people live on the platform surrounded by the drilling equipment, pumps and power plant. The platform also has living areas with places to sleep, eat and play.

A **research** ship is a floating laboratory. A large research ship needs a crew of up to twenty people. Thirty different scientists may also live and work on board.

scientist

Scientists study what lives in the water and on the sea floor. They also study how water moves in the oceans and how the oceans affect the **atmosphere**.

You could join the navy to have a life working at sea. You could also become a boatbuilder, engineer, lighthouse keeper, fisher, diver or even a ship's cook.

The crew of a submarine may stay submerged for weeks at a time.

Some boats are still built from wood.

Divers explore ocean life.

13

Ocean Highways

Ships used to be small and made of wood. Today they are large, powerful and made of steel. World trade depends on ships to carry goods around the world.

Ocean and sea routes are like water motorways. Ships follow special **shipping lanes** around the world. Each day, tankers carry oil from the Middle East to the rest of the world. Bulk carriers transport iron ore, coal, food and manufactured goods from one country to another. Cruise ships carry passengers on holiday.

With all this traffic, the shipping lanes can get very busy. So busy, there is a danger of ships colliding with each other! To solve the problem, ships have **radar** and **sonar** equipment. They also use radio waves sent via **satellite** to guide them. When the ships get close to land, lighthouses and marker **buoys** help them get to port safely.

tugboat

Tugboats guide large ships into port.

Icebreakers are special boats that can travel through ice fields.

Icebergs sometimes drift into shipping lanes. In 1912, nearly 1500 people drowned in the North Atlantic when a cruise ship, The Titanic, hit an iceberg and sank.

15

The Wild Sea

Some of the wildest storms on Earth begin at sea. When these storms hit land, they can cause terrible destruction.

Cyclones form over very warm seas. Water vapour rises and creates clouds. As the rising clouds get bigger, more warm air comes in from the bottom. Then the storm clouds start to spin.

These huge, spinning wind storms bring heavy rain and are very destructive. For ships at sea, cyclones are a great danger. When a cyclone hits land, it can cause terrible damage over a large area.

Tsunamis are giant waves caused by earthquakes in the seabed. When a tsunami gets close to land, the giant wave begins to crest and break. As the water gets shallower, the waves bump against the seabed and get higher and higher. Finally, the sea is sucked from the shore before the waves come rushing back as a giant wall of water.

16

Spinning cyclones can be seen from space.

Houses can be completely destroyed by cyclones.

GO FACTS

DID YOU KNOW?

A tsunami can travel across deep oceans as fast as a jet plane! The waves can be up to 65 metres high when they hit land.

Oceans in Trouble

Ocean pollution and overfishing are major problems. People need to work together to protect the oceans of the world.

The world's rivers and oceans are all connected. If chemical pollution from factories is dumped into rivers, it flows into the ocean. Whatever people put down a drain also ends up in the ocean. Even chemical sprays used on farms can seep through the ground and end up in the ocean. We cannot always see the pollution, but it can be deadly.

IF YOU HOOK A PELICAN
1. DO NOT CUT OR JERK LINE!
2. REEL BIRD IN SLOWLY
3. ASK ANOTHER FISHERMAN FOR HELP
4. GRASP BILL, CAREFULLY CONTAIN WINGS
5. REMOVE ALL LINES AND TACKLE
6. PUSH HOOK THRU, CUT BARB OFF, BACK OUT
7. DON'T FEED PELICANS IN FISHING AREAS
8. BIRDS WITH LINES ATTACHED DIE UNLESS RESCUED
REPORT INJURED BIRDS TO:

In 1989 a huge tanker, Exxon Valdez, struck a reef. It spilled 50 million litres of oil into the ocean. Oil spills like this are disastrous. The water is poisoned and sea creatures die. Animals also die when their feathers or fur get coated in oil.

Some laws have been passed to help protect the oceans. By working together, people can succeed in protecting the ocean and its wonderful wildlife.

Ships pollute the oceans by discharging waste.

DID YOU KNOW?
The Exxon Valdez oil spill covered more that 2 500 km of Alaskan shoreline. It killed at least 580 000 seabirds, and 5 500 sea and river otters.

This sea otter is covered in oil after an oil spill.

Enjoying the Sea

People enjoy activities such as swimming, surfing, scuba diving and boating. Simple rules help keep everyone safe.

At the beach, swimmers should follow the lifeguards' instructions. Surfers must stay away from swimming areas. If the waves are too rough or too big, don't swim.

Scuba divers must make sure their equipment is working properly before going on each dive. They also learn hand signals so they can communicate with other divers under water. No-one should dive alone.

There are special rules for people who like boating.

1 Make sure the boat is in good condition.

2 Plan your trip. Know where you are going and how long you will be. Tell someone else of your plans.

3 Check the weather forecast. Make sure it is safe boating weather.

4 Wear a life jacket.

5 Carry a first aid kit, torch, distress flares and a towrope. A radio that lets you talk to someone on shore is a good idea.

Surfers must stay
clear of swimmers.

People in boats have to
watch swimmers and
people snorkelling.

Sunscreen and shade protect
your skin from sunburn.

Using the Sea

Food

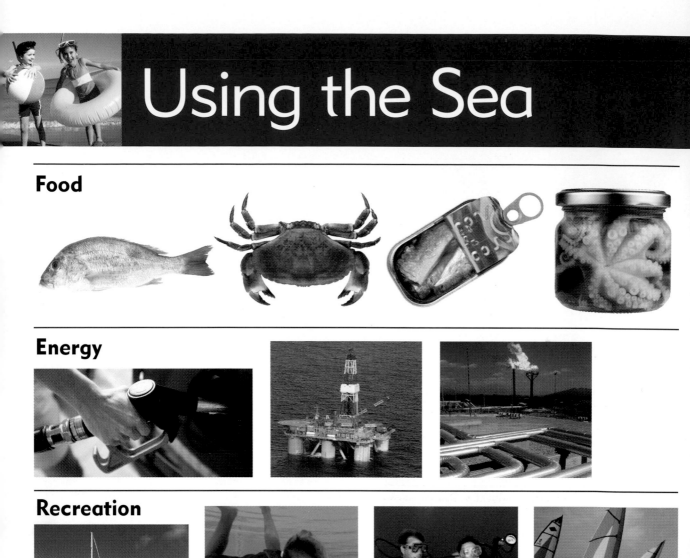

Energy

Recreation

Transportation

Glossary

atmosphere	the mixture of gases that surrounds Earth
buoy	an anchored marker that floats
fossil fuel	remains of plants and animals that have turned into oil and coal
geologist	someone who studies rocks
harvested	gathered grains or other live foods
radar	a positioning device that sends out radio waves and measures the time taken for the echo to return
satellite	an object that orbits Earth and sends and receives information
scuba	self contained underwater breathing apparatus
shipping lanes	regular routes that ships follow
sonar	equipment that uses sound waves to determine depth or position
tsunami	a large wave caused by an undersea earthquake
water pressure	pressure caused by the weight of water above

23

Index

School Days

Fiona Macdonald

W
FRANKLIN WATTS
NEW YORK • LONDON • SYDNEY

First published in 1998 by
Franklin Watts
96 Leonard Street
London EC2A 4RH

© Franklin Watts 1998

Franklin Watts Australia
14 Mars Road
Lane Cove
NSW 2006 Australia

Editor: Helen Lanz
Art Director: Robert Walster
Designer: Andrew Stagg
Consultant: Richard Dunn,
Ragged School Museum,
London

ISBN 0 7496 3084 1
Dewey Decimal
Classification Number: 371

Printed in Malaysia

Picture Credits

Cover: Mary Evans Picture
Library (main picture); Jill
Grey Collection/P. Millard
(bottom left); Franklin
Watts/Steve Shott (bottom
right)

Interior: Mary Evans Picture
Library pp. 7, 26; Getty
Images pp. 9t, 10, 25t, 27t,
29t; The Governers of
Christ's Hospital, Horsham
p. 11b; Jill Grey Collection/
P. Millard pp. 3, 8b, 9b, 15b,
25b; Reproduced by kind
permission of the The
American Museum in
Britain, Bath p. 12; Mansell
/Time Inc.pp. 11t, 16, 17t, 21t,
21b, 29b; Maria Montessori
Training Organisation,
AMI, London pp. 23b, 28t;
Popperfoto pp. 22, 23t;
Public Record Office Image
Library pp. 18b, 19, 20, 24,
28b; Science and Society
Picture Library pp. 4, 13t, 15t,
20; John Walmsley pp. 6, 8t,
13b, 14, 17b, 18t, 27b

CONTENTS

Introduction

Today, most schools are friendly and welcoming. At school, teachers help children to learn and discover many things.

A classroom in a *junior school* today. The children are working together on a maths project.

In the past, schools were not always as friendly. Teachers were often very **strict**.

TIME LINE

| 1900s | 1910s | 1920s | 1930s | 1940s |

A classroom in a junior school in the early 1900s. In the past, children were expected to sit still all day, be quiet and listen.

This book will tell you what schools were like long ago.

Look at this time line. It will tell you when the photographs showing the past were taken.

1950s   1960s   1970s   1980s   1990s   2000s

Slates, chalk and books

Today, schools have bright pictures on the walls, and a computer in most classrooms. There are art areas and story corners.

Today, children have many different types of equipment, such as computers, to help them learn.

This is a sand tray from the 1890s. Children used wooden pencils to write in the sand.

In the past, schools did not have as many ways to help learning, such as using books or computers, as they do now. Teachers wrote on blackboards using chalk. Children copied the words or numbers on to slates or into their sand trays.

TIME LINE

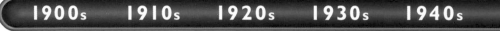

1900s   1910s   1920s   1930s   1940s

In this classroom in the late 1890s,
the boys are copying sums onto slates,
while the girls are practising reading.

In the past, children used
lead pencils or chalk to
write on slates like this.

Schools with a history

Some schools were set up hundreds of years ago and still survive today. Their buildings are very old.

In these old schools, **pupils** today sometimes wear the same style **uniform** as they did hundreds of years ago.

Children in an old school dormitory around 1900.

Some children *boarded* (stayed overnight). They slept in dormitories, big bedrooms they shared with other children.

TIME LINE

1900s   1910s   1920s   1930s   1940s

Boys at an old school called
Christ's Hospital. They are
marching off to lunch.

Pupils at Christ's Hospital
School in the 1990s.
Both girls and boys go
to Christ's Hospital now.
They wear the same
uniform as they did in
the past.

Learning to be ladies

Before about 1900, many girls from rich families did not go to school. Their mothers, or private teachers called 'governesses', taught them at home.

Girls did not study the same **subjects** as boys. Young ladies learned how to do beautiful needlework. They were taught good manners and how to be 'ladylike'.

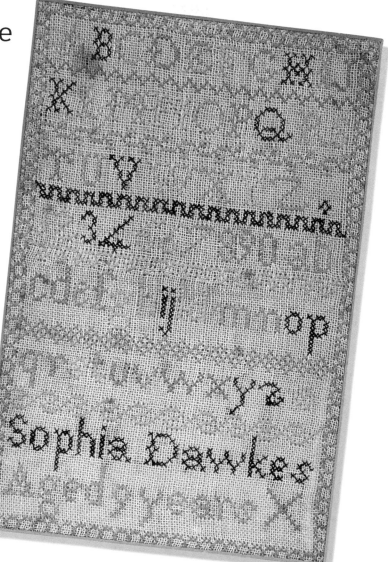

This sampler (a needlework picture) was made by a 9 year-old girl around 1900.

A young girl photographed around 1900 doing her needlework, while her governess reads.

In the past, girls learned to read and write, but they did not learn much about maths. Today, girls study all subjects at school.

Education for all

In the past, many children did not go to school. They never learned to read, write or do sums.

Then the government made laws that said all children had to go to school. Lots of new schools were built.

Today, all children over 5 years old have to go to school. They have to stay at school until they are at least 16 years old.

Some pupils stay on at school until they are 18 or 19 years old. They learn more about their favourite subjects.

TIME LINE

1900s   1910s   1920s   1930s   1940s

This school, photographed in 1906, was set up by the government for the children of the poor.

Some schools had workbooks for children to follow. This one is from around 1900.

10 CROWN PRIMER.—I.

Lesson F.

F. Ned has led the red ox.
G. he led it up to the shed.
H. let us go to the shed.
I. the red ox is fat; pat it.
J. yes, Ned has fed it.
K. is it wet in the shed?
L. if it is, do not go up.
M. go and get my bat.
N. I set it up in the shed.
O. Ned is to get my bat.

COLOURED DRAWING.

Private schools

In the past, many parents chose to send their children to **private schools**. They thought their children would learn more at these schools than at government schools.

A lesson at a private school for boys, 1920.

Parents had to pay to send their children to private schools. Only rich families could afford them.

Often, teachers at private schools wore old-fashioned hats (called mortar boards) and long coats (or gowns) like these.

(Below) Boys and girls at a private school today.

Today, most children go to government schools. They do not have to pay for their lessons.

But there are still a lot of private schools.

1950s   1960s   1970s   1980s   1990s   2000s

School sports

Sports and **PE** are fun. You can run, jump and climb.

Today sports clothes are stretchy and comfortable.

(Left) Children in the gym today. Compare this picture with the photograph below.

Boys exercising outside their school around 1930. They are all in neat rows, bending and stretching at the same time.

TIME LINE

1900s   1910s   1920s   **1930s**   1940s

In the past, sports and PE were much more strict.

Children could only move when their teacher told them. They wore much heavier clothes.

Girls in a gym, 1930. They are wearing a heavy dress, called a 'gym slip', and woollen stockings.

Village schools

In the past, country villages were often very small. This meant that village schools were also very small. Some had only one or two classes.

Children from a village school in 1933 play in fields near their school.

Children walking to a village school in the 1930s.

Children living in the country often had to walk a long way to school. Most people did not have cars, and there were few school buses.

Count the children to find out how many went to this small school in 1931.

New ways to learn

In the past, there was only one way of teaching. Children were made to copy information from books or from the blackboard, and learn it by heart.

In the early 1900s, teachers like Maria Montessori developed new ways of teaching.

A Montessori teacher in the 1940s helps children to learn by playing a game with wooden counters.

TIME LINE

1900s   1910s   1920s   1930s   **1940s**

Maria Montessori believed that children could learn by playing games and working together. This way of teaching tried to make learning fun.

(Above) This boy is learning to count by playing a game with number cards.

Children at a Montessori school today still use the same sort of equipment as Montessori schools in the past.

Working together is a common way to learn in many schools today.

Schools in wartime

During the **Second World War** (which lasted from 1939 to 1945) teachers and children had to be very brave.

The windows of this school were bricked up after it was hit by a bomb. But that did not stop lessons!

They had to carry on with lessons even though their schools were threatened by gas attacks or hit by bombs.

TIME LINE

1900s 1910s 1920s 1930s **1940s**

Children outside a school,
1941. They are wearing
their gas masks in case of
a poison gas attack.

A wartime gas mask.
It covered the eyes and
the nose, and protected
people from poison gas.

1950s   1960s   1970s   1980s   1990s   2000s

New schools

In the 1950s, many new schools were built. They were made of new materials, such as metal and concrete.

Many of these new schools had large windows. This made the classrooms light and sunny.

Inside the new schools, pupils often still sat at old-fashioned desks, arranged in rows.

TIME LINE

1900s   1910s   1920s   1930s   1940s

This *secondary school*
was built in the 1950s.
It is made of metal and
concrete. Some walls
are almost all glass.

This school today is
a mixture of old and
new buildings. The oldest
buildings are on the right.

1950s   1960s   1970s   1980s   1990s   2000s

Useful words

boarded: when pupils did not go home at the end of the day or at weekends, but stayed at school.

junior school: in Britain, these are schools for children who are between 7 and 11 years old.

Montessori: a way of teaching children based on the beliefs of Maria Montessori.

PE: Physical Education. All the sports, games and gym you do at school.

private schools: schools where parents pay for their children to have lessons.

pupil: a person who is being taught at school or college.

28

Second World War: the war that lasted from 1939 to 1945. It is called a world war because so many countries took part.

secondary school: in Britain, secondary schools are for children who are between 11 and 18 years old.

strict: when there are many rules to follow and you get into trouble for breaking any of them.

subjects: different topics to study at school or college, such as maths, science or English.

uniform: special clothes that are worn to show that you go to a certain school or do a certain job.

29

Index